Dear Female Leader

30 Days of Encouragement for Female Leaders (and the Women Who Think They Aren't)

Mandy B. Anderson and Raychel Perman

Copyright © 2022 Mandy Anderson (penname Mandy B. Anderson) and Raychel Perman

Published in the United States by RAYMA Team Media, a division of RAYMA Team, LLC. www.raymateam.com

1st Edition

Copyright in Bismarck, North Dakota

All rights reserved.

No portion of this book may be reproduced, stored in a retrieval system, or transmitted in any form or by any means – electronic, mechanical, photocopy, recording, scanning, or any other – except for brief quotations in critical reviews or articles, without the prior written permission of the publisher.

For permissions contact: info@raymateam.com or visit www.raymateam.com.

Paperback Print ISBN: 978-1-7379099-5-8

Cover Design by: Mandy Anderson

Photography by: Jacy Jo Photography

Introduction

This book is for the woman who proudly owns the fact that she is a leader, and for the one who often thinks to herself, "But I'm not a leader, I'm just here being my best self."

It breaks our hearts when women fail to see themselves as leaders, especially when they are already leading but it's hidden under the guise of "volunteering" or "mom duties."

Women are the ones who take the initiative to change communities for the better.

Women are the ones who help empower their female friends and support their businesses.

Women are the ones who rally around another woman and help her get the help and support she needs in desperate circumstances.

Women are the ones who take the first step in healing their marriages and changing their financial future.

Women are leaders. Period.

Coming to terms with our leadership as women is something we understand well. We started our first company together in 2014. Bright-eyed and full of hope we set off on the journey of entrepreneurship with heads full of dreams and hearts bursting with naivete. Like all women carrying the torch of entrepreneur before us, we too had a story that led us to starting our life coaching company. But, unlike many partnerships ours didn't start the day we decided to go into business together. Our journey began nearly three decades before.

HERE'S OUR STORY:

We met in the summer between fifth and sixth grade, at a small Bible Camp smack dab in the middle of North Dakota. We bonded over a love of singing and escaping group activities. We saw no earthly reason to participate in relays that consisted of passing oranges between our knees. Can you blame us?

We would hide in our cabin with two other friends while Mandy did the breathing treatments she required to keep her lungs as healthy as possible. Mandy was born with Cystic Fibrosis, and it was the best excuse ever to get out of activities we didn't want to do! We would gush over the cute boys, talk about our budding faith, practice singing harmony with Disney songs and old hymns, process family and friend drama, and dream about the future.

Back then success meant becoming a singing sensation like Point of Grace. In case you didn't grow up in Evangelical Christianity in the 90s, Point of Grace was an all-female contemporary Christian musical group. They were a quartet that sang four-part harmony, and we wanted nothing more than to follow in their famous footsteps.

Eventually we realized that becoming a famous music group wasn't in the cards for us. But that dream of doing something together never really died. We had many conversations over the years that started with, "wouldn't it be cool if..."

In 2011, we found ourselves finally living in the same town. I had just graduated college and was working as a Certified Biblical Counselor at a local church; and, simultaneously working on building a new career as a Professional Life and Health Coach.

In 2012 life happened in a way neither of us saw coming. That year, Mandy would spend 22 days in the hospital fighting to stay alive. It was the perfect storm brought on by unresolved grief, trauma from a house fire where she lost everything and walking by faith for a supernatural healing. Her risky decisions almost cost her the successful life she dreamed of.

While Mandy was fighting for her life, Raychel would face severe Postpartum OCD as she welcomed their third child. Anxiety and intrusive thoughts robbed her of her mental and emotional health for nearly a year. In the background she battled against the war that alcoholism had dropped on her front door. Her marriage was falling apart at the seams, and she was drowning in the pressure of it all.

During that time, we often found ourselves sitting on the big blue couch in Raychel's living room processing life. This wasn't any old piece of furniture. It turned into a magical place where we would snuggle into its faded cushions to laugh, cry, eat, and dream again. It was during those times we first learned how to rise out of the ashes of our circumstances and harness our resilience, authenticity, motivation, and assertiveness. We grieved what was lost while simultaneously saying yes to a brighter future. Even when everything seemed dead. We choose to plant precious seeds of faith, hope, and determination.

In 2013 we started building a lay counseling ministry to provide services to the staff and parishioners at a local church. We had big dreams for the future that included staff training and yearly events for women. We knew we didn't go through 2012 for nothing. We would turn our pain into purpose.

A few days into 2014, everything changed. And we found ourselves once again on that much-loved couch processing life. Drunk on wine and revenge, convinced someone was trying to steal our dream, an idea transpired. We decided to take authority over our future and build from the ashes. That night our first LLC Big Blue Couch Coaching was born.

We saw lots of success with that first company. Sold out events. Traveling for speaking engagements. Publishing our own books and coaching content. We even had a weekly spot on a local television morning show for almost three years straight. We made our first 50k and were well on our way to having our first six-figure year. We tasted business success for the first time, and it was good.

When Raychel filed for divorce in 2017, Mandy often steered the business ship. It was a skill we learned all the way back in 2012. When one of us was weak, the other was strong. Like a tiny herd of momma elephants in the wild, we learned how to surround each other and kick up dirt when the other was in distress. Business thrived amid personal tragedy.

Something changed as we approached our fifth anniversary in 2019. The business wasn't successful like it was before. Numbers dwindled. Sales slowed. And we were constantly in the red. What once fit like a favorite comfy sweater started to feel like a pair of pants that shrunk in the dryer. We were outgrowing our own company.

So, we lit the match and burned everything down. We rose from the ashes with a new look, a new name, and a new mission. RAYMA Team, LLC was born.

The current mission is to revolutionize how leadership development is done. Our name - RAYMA - is more than just a combination of our names. It stands for the five foundational qualities that form the focus for our signature RAYMA Foundations™ leadership trainings:

- Resilience
- Authenticity
- Yes mindset
- Motivation
- Assertiveness

Now, we are telling the stories we never told before – the lessons we learned from our journeys as leaders.

OUR PROFESSIONAL EXPERIENCE:

Prior to starting our company in 2014, we both had leadership experience as volunteer leaders in various church settings, as well as in the marketplace.

Raychel had a decade long career in the spa industry where she trained and hired Estheticians as the Lead Esthetician. At the same time she was running a spa, she also got her degree in Psychology and Christian Counseling while raising two small children with a husband who traveled frequently for work.

Mandy was a trusted leader in the hospitality industry as a Wedding & Event Planner where she often managed up to seven weddings per weekend. She eventually became a PR Director at an extended-stay hotel, where she helped them become one of the Top 10 hotels in the country for that hotel chain.

Several years ago, women told us that they couldn't relate to most leadership training because it was written by men and felt outdated. We decided to do something about it and went to work creating a solution that was relevant for all genders and walks of life, not just women.

Our RAYMA Foundations™ signature leadership training combines effective life coaching techniques with timeless leadership principles to develop quality leaders with strong teams and healthy coping skills.

When you work with us, you're getting over a decade of experience in leadership development, business building, and knowing how to lead your team well when life happens - without sacrificing your health, family, or the hobbies that bring you joy and fulfillment.

WHY WE WROTE THIS BOOK:

We decided to write this book to encourage women to rise up as the leaders they can be and are. We know when a woman defines leadership for herself, and overcomes the obstacles keeping her stuck, she can become unstoppable. She just needs the confidence and accountability to stick it out.

So, dear friend, as you go through these pages, know that these letters are written from our hearts to yours. Pretend we are your Certified Life Coaches (because we are) and that we are writing these letters directly to you. Sometimes the daily letter is from one of us, and sometimes it is from both of us.

Take notes, come back to this booklet often, and above all always remember:

You were placed on this earth for such a time as this, and you are fully equipped to lead and influence others in a positive way.

Much love and with grace and grit,
~Coach Mandy and Coach Raychel

Day 1

Stop Apologizing for Your Feminine Leadership Traits

Truth Statement®:

I am proud of the feminine traits that I have. I will no longer hide my compassion, empathy, creativity, or vulnerability. I will not devalue my self-worth. I choose to hold my head high and be proud of myself.

Dear Female Leader:

Stop apologizing for your feminine leadership traits. Hold your head up high and own them.

What are Feminine Leadership Traits? They are traits such as:

- Compassion
- Empathy
- Creativity
- Vulnerability
- Self-worth

As a society, we've been conditioned to believe that the feminine leadership traits are weak, so we often apologize for them.

Stop that!

Girl, it's time to be proud of your feminine leadership traits! No more apologizing and making excuses when people disrespect your leadership.

Hold your head high and own them!

~Coach Mandy and Coach Raychel

Notes to myself about today's encouragement:

Day 2

Lead The Next Generation Of Women Without Pettiness

Truth Statement®:

I will share wisdom and guidance with women younger than me. I choose to have eyes to see the best in them.

Dear Female Leader:

We need you to lead the women younger than you without being threatened by their youthfulness. We need you to speak wisdom and guidance into them without being petty.

I was only 23 when my male boss came into the townhome rental office I managed and told me that the other female co-workers thought I was "intimidating." I remember being so confused about what I had done wrong...

When they wanted me to evict the tenants that were months behind their rent and not able to keep up with any payment plans, I found the courage to do the hard thing. I was so scared to be the bad guy, but I did it with as much compassion as I could.

When my boss wanted me to fix the mess from the past rental manager and get those units rented, I did it. I worked hard and I asked questions, and I did what needed to be done to meet that goal.

And there I was, getting in trouble because the other women on the team found me intimidating. Mind you, these other two women were 20-30 years older than me. Instead of recognizing their leadership and influence to help me grow as a young woman in the workforce, they belittled me and made up stories.

Decades later, I see this happening to women in the workplace often. Other women feel threatened by you, so they try to belittle you and disrespect you. The way women treat each other in the workplace can sometimes be worse than the gender equality issues we face as female leaders!

This is why I'm so passionate about helping women step into the shoes of Fearless Feminine Leadership. Because we need women leaders that know how to lead younger women and speak wisdom and guidance into them without being petty.

We also need women who know how to call out the backstabbing BS and gossip that happens in the workplace and create a strong, unified team that honors people and knows how to be mature. And we desperately need to offer leadership training to the young women that don't hold a title of leader yet but have a strong desire to grow.

Be this kind of leader, dear friend.

~Coach Mandy

Notes to myself about today's encouragement:

Day 3

You Need Confidence And Competence

Truth Statement®:

Confidence will take me far. And growing in my competence through continued training and accountability will help me be great.

Dear Female Leader:

You need confidence and competence to succeed.

You need the grit to say "Actually, I can. Watch me," and the grace to know you need to sharpen your skills.

And you need someone in your corner offering accountability, training, and support.

I used to think I could succeed without the help of others. Because of this, I sabotaged much of my own personal and professional growth, and my ability to lead like a rockstar, in my twenties. Age and lots of hard life experiences (like filing for divorce and health challenges I never saw coming!) have taught me the error of my ways and I easily look for others who know more than me and can give me wisdom and perspective.

Confidence can take you far as a leader. But growing in your competence through continued training and accountability will give you the foundation you need when you feel shaky, scared, and indecisive.

Confidence and competence are what confident rockstar women need to lead! What you don't need is more rah-rah sisterhood toxic positivity BS.

~Coach Raychel

Notes to myself about today's encouragement:

Day 4

Act Like A Female Leader

Truth Statement®:

My feminine leadership qualities make me strong.

Dear Female Leader:

You don't have to act like a man to be a great leader. All you need to do is step into your own feminine leadership qualities with confidence.

Your feminine leadership qualities are what make you strong!

Lead well.

~Coach Mandy & Coach Raychel

Notes to myself about today's encouragement:

Day 5

#####

Let Go Of The Fear Of Being A Bitch

Truth Statement®:

Today, I choose to be a Fearless Feminine Leader. I will believe that my voice is powerful. I will believe that my leadership matters. I can't mess this up. I am fully capable of learning new skills. I can lead well and be a work in progress at the same time. My experience is enough to start now. I can deal with and accept whatever judgment comes my way. Every day I get to begin again. People want what I have. People love to work with me. I am blessed and highly favored. I am worthy of respect. I am a Fearless Feminine Leader.

Dear Female Leader:

Stop being afraid of the people that think you are a bitch. Hold your head high and show up as the intelligent, mature leader that you are.

The number one fear that women in leadership have is that people will think you are a bitch if you lead confidently. Let's talk about that...

Here's what it looks like when you're afraid to lead because someone might call you a bitch:

- You don't speak up in meetings unless someone asks you to.

- You avoid situations where you have to self-promote or highlight your accomplishments.

- You hide online - meaning you either don't post anything or you share everyone else's stuff, so it looks like you're showing up.

- You coddle people and over-explain in a sugar-coated way so that they don't get mad at you.

- You don't stand up for yourself when you feel disrespected.

Sound familiar? It's time to change this and step into Fearless Feminine Leadership! A Fearless Feminine

Leader understands that if someone thinks she's a bitch, it says more about them than it does about her.

A Fearless Feminine Leader knows how to have self-respect so she can stand up for herself when others disrespect her.

A Fearless Feminine Leader speaks up confidently and chooses her words wisely, so others listen when she speaks. She learns communication secrets and knows how to bring unity in a team when there is discord.

A Fearless Feminine Leader knows when and how to self-promote and is proud of her accomplishments. She knows what she brings to the table and how she can help the organization she works for and the people she leads.

It's time to be fearless.

~Coach Mandy and Coach Raychel

Notes to myself about today's encouragement:

Day 6

You Teach Others How To Treat You By What You Allow

Truth Statement®:

Respect starts with me. I choose to have self-respect, and to respect others as I want to be respected.

Dear Female Leader:

You are always teaching people how to treat you, and others, by what you allow. For instance:

- If you let people disrespect you by constantly rolling their eyes at you or blowing up in anger at you, then you've taught them that it's okay not to respect you.

- If you reply to client messages at all hours of the day, then you've taught them that not respecting your work hours is okay.

- If you wait to start the team meeting until everyone arrives - ten minutes late - then you've taught them to not respect your time or anyone else's.

Respect starts with you and there are a million different ways that you allow people to disrespect you.

~Coach Mandy

Notes to myself about today's encouragement:

Day 7

•••••

Your Confidence Grows When You Build Your Faith

Truth Statement®:

I choose to have faith today. I have faith in myself and my abilities. I have faith that things are working out for me even if I can't see it yet.

Dear Female Leader:

Your confidence grows when you build your faith. I tell my private coaching clients all the time:

Your confidence grows when you build your faith - faith in yourself and faith in something bigger. You need faith in what you cannot see! Your greatest strength comes from inside.

Have faith in what you cannot see. Slow down so you can lead with conviction and courage. Your faith inspires the people you lead to walk by faith, too.

~Coach Raychel

Notes to myself about today's encouragement:

Day 8

Take The Time To Understand

Truth Statement®:

I will let go of my pride and ego so I can consider the viewpoints of other people. Understanding others helps me be a better leader.

Dear Female Leader:

You cannot lead in the tension of strong beliefs and differing opinions if you are constantly defending your viewpoints and refusing to get understanding.

Let go of your pride and ego. Let go of the desire to be right, or to be seen as the hero amid differing opinions.

Over the last few years, our society has come to see people with different or opposing views as people who are the enemy. This must STOP.

People who see things differently are not your enemy! They are PEOPLE who see the world differently - and that's okay. It's necessary.

Things are not always as black and white as you've been led to believe they are. Wherever you will find people, you will find a variety of life experiences that have shaped people's viewpoints and this is why you must find the courage to handle strong beliefs and differing opinions with honor and respect.

The key to all of this is in your ability to listen and understand.

As a Leader, you've got to develop the skills of listening to and understanding every person you encounter. Not just the ones who share your beliefs and opinions. Not just the ones you get along with well. Not just the ones you admire or want to schmooze. Everyone.

~Coach Mandy

Notes to myself about today's encouragement:

Day 9

Manage Your Time Wisely

Truth Statement®:

I owe it to myself, and those I lead, to manage my time wisely.

Dear Female Leader:

Your time is valuable and so is your peace of mind. You owe it to yourself, and those you lead, to manage your time wisely.

Busy women (especially entrepreneurs and corporate leaders) often have a common problem of scheduling themselves in chaotic ways. You find yourself jumping around to different tasks that don't make sense. You can't focus on any task completely from start to finish and nothing gets done.

If this sounds familiar, I highly suggest that you try batch scheduling. For example:

- If you take clients, make sure it's on certain days or times of the day (example - Tuesdays & Wednesdays in the mornings or afternoons).

- Don't schedule meetings and client sessions willy-nilly because you will break focus every time you have to leave a project for a meeting and vice versa.

- Or schedule mornings for personal and family tasks and afternoons for work tasks (and vice versa).

Sometimes I even batch schedule analytic tasks together and creative tasks together.

Experiment with it to find what works best for you. This will help you better manage your time and feel more balanced, peaceful, and accomplished.

~Coach Raychel

Notes to myself about today's encouragement:

Day 10

Respect Should Not Be Earned

Truth Statement®:

Today I will choose to respect every person that I meet because everyone is worthy of respect. Even me.

Dear Female Leader:

Every person is worthy of respect. Even you.

Ever heard the saying "respect is earned?" That's BS. It's more nuanced than that and we need to talk about it, because there is a difference between respect and trust when it comes to leadership. There's a certain level of respect in leadership that should not be earned - it should be given.

Here's why: Every single human being is worthy of being respected no matter what their title or position; no matter their gender, race, or age. All humans are worthy of their rights and privacy being respected! All humans are worthy of being treated with kindness and consideration!

This idea that a leader needs to earn respect is a bunch of BS. A leader should get a certain level of respect no matter her age, race, or gender! Likewise, a leader should give respect to others no matter age, gender, race, or position in an organization or community.

Here's where this idea that respect is earned, not given, goes wrong: People use the words trust and respect as though they are synonyms. They are not.

Trust is what is actually earned. It takes time to get to know someone's character enough to trust them or not. But *respect* - that should be given and allowed to grow deeper with time.

Be the type of leader who gives respect to others regardless of if it is given in return. Turn the tables and learn how to respectfully disagree with emotional resilience and wisdom instead of gossiping and always being defensive.

Be the Fearless Feminine Leader who knows how to sow respect with everyone she meets.

~Coach Mandy

Notes to myself about today's encouragement:

Day 11

You Can Do Hard Things

Truth Statement®:

I can do hard things. I can pivot. I can come out of hardships stronger than when I went in. I will not give up.

Dear Female Leader:

You can do hard things. You can.

And I promise you that the woman who is waiting on the other side of your healing is worth fighting for. Promise.

I know what it's like to have your world turned upside down in an instant. I know how it feels to suddenly pivot and have to create a new normal.

In the last five years, I have had to recover from a messy divorce, heal from decades of trauma, manage my anxiety depression and PTSD, and re-create a new story for myself and my family.

You can pivot. I believe you can come out of hardships stronger than you went in. Don't give up.

~Coach Raychel

Notes to myself about today's encouragement:

Day 12

You're Not Alone

Truth Statement®:

I am not alone when things feel heavy. It's okay for me to question things.

Dear Female Leader:

It's okay if today feels heavy. You're not alone in that feeling.

It's okay if you are questioning a lot of things. In fact, that's healthy.

Give yourself some grace, treat yourself to your favorite drink, and journal or watch your favorite movie. You don't have to fix everything when you feel this way. Learn to be okay with the heavy and lean into processing things in bite-sized pieces.

~Coach Mandy

Notes to myself about today's encouragement:

Day 13

•••••

You. Can. Leave.

Truth Statement®:
I can leave if I must.

Dear Female Leader:

You can leave *for* the children.

There are many reasons a woman stays in an abusive relationship, and all are valid. Including staying because of the kids. However, you can leave *for* them, too. I did.

I wanted my kids to see something different. I wanted them to have a chance to heal their childhood wounds while they were still children. I didn't want them to think what their parents had was healthy or something to emulate.

I stayed for many reasons. But I left *for* them.

It's a valid reason to go. Full stop.

~Coach Raychel

P.S. This letter might not be speaking directly to your circumstances. If that's the case, read it again so that you can build empathy for the women that are in the situation where they need to decide to stay or go. But also, don't be afraid to apply what you need to for yourself when it comes to the topic of leaving any type of toxic environment.

Notes to myself about today's encouragement:

Day 14

Define What Makes You Feel Your Best

Truth Statement®:
I refuse to lose myself in my leadership role.

Dear Female Leader:

You get to define what makes you feel like your best feminine leader self. Let's chat about this for a second...

I was showing my French manicure to my niece the other day when she said, "Your nails are only half done."

I went on to explain that it was on purpose. That this was called a French manicure and that I liked it because it was simple, yet classy.

That's when her mom spoke up and said something along the lines of, "Wow. The fact that she has never seen a French manicure is quite telling. I used to get them all the time - they were my go-to style."

Self-care is an important leadership skill that is often the first to go when deadlines and the pressure to succeed pile up.

I get it - I do it too! Oftentimes my version of a lack of self-care looks like:

- Not getting haircuts so my hair ends up super long and in a messy bun and then I just feel yucky.

- Not taking time for a pedicure or manicure. (I went without for 5 years! Just getting back into the habit now.)

- Not getting a massage to release the tension headaches. (This is currently at the top of my list.)

- Working 24/7 and not taking a break because I forget how to have fun.

When you notice any of these symptoms (and others) creeping up, it's time to do something about it. Don't lose yourself in your role as a leader.

~Coach Mandy

Notes to myself about today's encouragement:

Day 15

Lead By Example

Truth Statement®:

Sickness and grief do not disqualify me from leading.

Dear Female Leader:

Become the Victor of your circumstances. Lead by example when sickness or hard times come.

Yes, you can still lead fearlessly even when you don't feel well. Sickness and grief do not disqualify you as a leader.

Be vulnerable and honest.

Establish healthy boundaries.

Boldly take care of yourself so that you can empower others to take care of themselves, too.

Your leadership matters whether you feel good or not.

~Coach Mandy and Coach Raychel

Notes to myself about today's encouragement:

Day 16

Focus On One Skill At A Time

Truth Statement®:

I will be laser-focused about the skill I am cultivating so I can see new sprouts in due time.

Dear Female Leader:

It's okay to focus on growing one skill at a time.

Why does a farmer plant only one main crop at a time in each field? So she can concentrate on what that seed needs to grow. She can get specific on what nutrients that plant needs. And she will be able to target the weeds and mulch to give those seeds a fighting chance.

When it comes to growing your leadership skills, you need to concentrate on one field at a time.

I used to either ignore my fields or go nuts and try to grow ALL THE THINGS! But, in all honesty, both methods sucked!

I couldn't grow as fast or as healthy as I wanted when I was wasn't focused on one skill at a time. I had to get laser-focused on the belief or behavior I wanted to cultivate in that season of my life.

What do you want to cultivate in this season of your life? Be precise and laser-focused about it and you will see new sprouts in due time.

~Coach Raychel

Notes to myself about today's encouragement:

Day 17

Your Title Doesn't Matter

Truth Statement®:

I am a leader no matter what my title is. My determination to lead others is what makes me a leader.

Dear Female Leader:

Having a title doesn't make you a leader. You become a leader with your determination to lead others and yourself well. That's how you become a Rockstar Leader in your life and your career.

I'd be lying if I told you that being a Fearless Feminine Leader was going to be easy, though. It's not as simple as "just pulling on your big-girl panties!" You'll need to put on your best ass-kicking shoes and daily kick your fears – and the lies and labels - to the curb so you can lead well!

It's going to take some heart work. It demands more courage and bravery than you've ever mustered up before. It begs you to become the type of leader who is resilient, authentic, has a yes mindset, is self-motivated, and assertive. And the secret to overcoming all the fears and lies so you can be this type of leader is this: You need a mentor who's been there and can guide you.

You can't do it alone. There is great value in finding a mentor and coach that can encourage you, give you guidance, and offer valid feedback without judgment.

Every Female Leader needs a mentor – even you.

~Coach Mandy

Notes to myself about today's encouragement:

Day 18

What They Said Doesn't Matter

Truth Statement®:

I get to choose which words I will believe about myself.

Dear Female Leader:

What they said about you doesn't matter.

As women, we all have this in common: Lies & labels torment our minds and have us fooled! But... we get to choose what we will believe.

Let today be the day that you draw a line in the sand and choose to stop rehashing the hurt!

You are enough because your Creator says so.

You are smarter than you give yourself credit for.

You are placed on the earth for such a time as this!

No more believing the lies!

~Coach Raychel

Notes to myself about today's encouragement:

Day 19

Focus On What You Bring To The Table

Truth Statement®:

Today I will lead with what I am good at. I will be confident and let go of my insecurities.

Dear Female Leader:

When you introduce yourself in any type of networking group, stop leading with what you're not good at. Focus on what you bring to the table. Focus on what you love, what you bring to the table – what you are great at! Be confident and let go of the insecurities.

The other day I was at a networking event for women. It was a small group of seven of us...

As we went around the table introducing ourselves, I noticed an interesting trend. Half of the women introduced themselves like this:

"Hi, I'm so and so and I own my own business, (or just started a network marketing company, work full time and am building a business on the side). I'm excited to be here because I really don't know what I'm doing. I love the company I work for but I'm not good at sales or social media. I'm not like this other company, I'm not great at that. In fact, this is the issue I'm currently having..."

Usually, they ended up rambling about their struggles for another five minutes before finishing up with, "I'm sorry! I'm rambling so you go next!"

We need to talk about this because it happens more often than you realize. I've done it, you've done it. It's a thing that women do especially when they feel insecure and unsure about what they do.

I'm here to help you become a Fearless Feminine Leader who is confident in what you bring to the table! So, here's a few tips to stop leading your introduction with what you're not good at. INSTEAD follow this format...

- Your name and company.

- What product or service you provide.

- Tell a short client testimonial or highlight quickly why you are great at what you do with a relevant story.

- Recap your name and company and share a business card.

And then move along.

Ninety seconds to two minutes tops. Practice it beforehand so you're ready and it rolls off your tongue.

Networking groups should not be your therapy or coaching group. They are the place where you meet new people and build connections.

~Coach Mandy

Notes to myself about today's encouragement:

Day 20

You Are Human

Truth Statement®:

I am human. When I make mistakes, I will remember that I can try again tomorrow.

Dear Female Leader:

Remember that you are human.

If today left you feeling like you are letting people down, stop beating yourself up and remember that you are human.

And you can try again tomorrow.

~Coach Raychel

Notes to myself about today's encouragement:

Day 21

Your Fears Should Motivate You To Take Action

Truth Statement®:

When I feel afraid, I will take the time to identify my fear and learn more about it. This will help me take action.

Dear Female Leader:

The fears you have as a leader should motivate you to take action - not surrender.

Fear makes you act a certain way. It will cause you to set easy goals and dreams only - if you set any goals at all. If you are a person of faith, and you are full of fear, you will refuse to act when God asks you to. You will be too scared to make decisions, causing you to miss opportunities that might never come back again.

It's time to make a change if you've been operating like this. This is not what Fearless Feminine Leaders do!

From this point forward, make it your goal to identify how fear affects you. Knowing how fear affects you can help you identify your patterns – and that's a powerful skill that every female leader needs to know!

~Coach Mandy

Notes to myself about today's encouragement:

Day 22

You Are Qualified

Truth Statement®:

I choose to believe that I am qualified to lead and influence the people in my life in a positive way.

Dear Female Leader:

You are qualified to influence and lead the people in your life.

Sometimes you just need to be reminded of who you are. So let me remind you that you are tougher than you think and smarter than they made you believe. The truth is you are a Rockstar boss who is brave and qualified to influence and lead the people in your life.

I know it takes time to believe it. It took me years to believe this, and I did it by changing my mindset. I replaced lies like I was weak, worthless, and overlooked with the truth of my divine feminine power.

This is why I take my job to remind you of who YOU are seriously. My clients know I'm their biggest fan and watching them take their power back and take the big leaps is my favorite.

You are qualified. Believe it.

~Coach Raychel

Notes to myself about today's encouragement:

Day 23

Become Self-Aware

Truth Statement®:

I will dig deep so I can become self-aware.

Dear Female Leader:

Embrace the principle of self-awareness and evaluate your core values often.

Contrary to popular leadership training, discovering your core values isn't a once-and-done thing. Core values take different priority depending on the season you are in and the person you are becoming. As you grow, your priorities change. Your core values will evolve, too.

You might even discover some new ones that you didn't think would be there once you grow into the person that can handle that value!

Fearless Feminine Leaders embrace the leadership principle of self-awareness. They work harder on themselves than anything else so that they can help others do the same. They face their fears of being disrespected and seeming like a bitch.

They confront the BS thinking that "respect is earned," because they recognize that every human being is deserving of respect without condition.

They dig deep and know the value they bring.

~Coach Mandy

Notes to myself about today's encouragement:

Day 24

Develop A Strong Mindset

Truth Statement®:

Yes, I can.

Dear Female Leader:

You will believe 100% of the words you tell yourself. This is why developing a strong mindset as a leader is so important.

The women who have the greatest impact on the world around them are the ones who push past the barriers in their own mind.

The ones who know how to be their own biggest cheerleader when nobody else is around to pump them up. Those are the women that are powerful, fearless leaders.

Why?

Because they know how to overcome their own demons and they don't let fear stop them.

This is the type of woman I aim to be. Whether it's running a 5k or speaking on a stage in front of a crowd of 1,000 people - whenever I feel like I can't, I start saying this mantra:

Yes, I can.

Yes, I can.

Yes, I can.

Over and over again I repeat it in my mind or whisper it out loud. And eventually Yes, I can, becomes Yes, I did.

~Coach Mandy

Notes to myself about today's encouragement:

Day 25

Lead From Your Heart

Truth Statement®:

I will stand firm in who I am and lead from my heart.

Dear Female Leader:

Don't base your leadership style on the opinions of your haters. Be you.

Lead from your heart. Stand firm in who you are. Respect everyone and have healthy boundaries.

~Coach Mandy

Notes to myself about today's encouragement:

Day 26

Set The Boundary

Truth Statement®:

I get to decide how I am treated. Therefore, I will learn to set healthy boundaries.

Dear Female Leader:

They will call you difficult when they can't manipulate you any longer.

First you set the boundary. Then you enforce the consequences. The part that trips us up is often the 2nd step. As high-level women leaders we want to look like we have it all together, but our relationships are often crumbling in the background. If you want respect, you must enforce the boundaries you set.

I sucked at this for years in my personal relationships. I was the people-pleasing scape goat in my family of origin, so I naturally brought that into my relationships as an adult. It wasn't until I started to work harder on my own personal growth that it started to change. I did that by working with counselors and coaches.

My biggest flex was when I enforced the consequence and filed for divorce in 2017 after the boundaries were crossed and the separation failed. I've been walking out boundaries and consequences in my personal and professional life ever since.

I get to decide how I'm treated.

So do you!

~Coach Raychel

Notes to myself about today's encouragement:

Day 27

•••••

You Are The Answer To Someone's Prayers

Truth Statement®:

I will start leading right where I am at. I believe someone has been praying for the leadership I can offer.

Dear Female Leader:

You are the answer to someone's prayers.

The day I learned to respect myself and my dreams is the day I stepped into leadership. I realized then that you can't lead someone if you haven't learned to first lead yourself.

I had to stop believing the lie that told me I wasn't a leader yet because I didn't have a team or a title.

I had to stop repeating the narrative that I wasn't good enough.

And I had to confront the mindset of "who am I that I should think I can lead?"

I had to start believing some truth:

- My leadership matters.

- My legacy matters.

- I have solutions that people need and I've learned lessons that can help people.

- And I had to believe that I was the answer to someone's prayers. All I had to do was start leading, right where I was.

There is untapped potential inside of you that will shock you with excitement when you finally step into it.

You have wisdom that others need to hear. You have hard-learned lessons to share that can help someone else not feel so alone. Your story matters and someone needs to hear it.

It's time to become the Fearless Feminine Leader that you have been put on this earth to be.

Your leadership matters. It's time to start leading right where you are.

~Coach Mandy

Notes to myself about today's encouragement:

Day 28

Speak Up For Yourself

Truth Statement®:

I will learn to speak up for myself in moments where I feel uncomfortable, unheard, or disrespected.

Dear Female Leader:

It's okay to speak up for yourself.

"This is making me uncomfortable - please stop bringing it up."

That's what I said to a gentleman that made some inappropriate comments during a conversation. His reply was, "You don't have to be so passive aggressive."

Here's the thing that all Female Leaders need to come to terms with. Some men cannot handle direct communication, so they will try to make you out to be an irrational, emotional woman. Not every man - but some. Dudes like that are stuck in a patriarchal mindset of sexism that they may or may not be aware of.

So how do you handle it when something like this happens?

Hold your head up high and stand up for yourself!

This might look like saying the words that I did, or it might look like putting down a personal boundary of not being around this person or doing business with them.

If you're not at the point of confidently expressing your boundaries with words, take some time to journal and process why something like that bothers you.

Ask yourself: Why did I allow someone to treat me like that?

And then brainstorm ideas of words you could say that would make you feel proud of yourself for standing up for your own self-respect.

Being able to handle this in the moment takes practice, especially if you've never stood up for yourself like this before.

~Coach Mandy

Notes to myself about today's encouragement:

Day 29

Trust Your Gut

Truth Statement®:
I will trust my intuition today.

Dear Female Leader:

Trust your gut and jump.

"How do I know if this is the right choice to make?"

That's the universal question that every female coaching client asks me. I tell my clients when they are wrestling with this question to make a pros and cons list, to sleep on it, to journal, pray, talk about it during a session, and look for a sign. But ultimately you have to trust your gut and jump.

Your ability to trust your intuition and make a leap of faith is what makes you brave and a leader worth following. Will your curiosity always lead to success? Maybe. Maybe not. The point is that you jumped. You took the risk. You won't ever live with regret about this... and you will one day be so grateful you did.

~Coach Raychel

Notes to myself about today's encouragement:

Day 30

You Have Permission to Grow

Truth Statement®:

I have permission to step away from those things that no longer fit.

Dear Female Leader:

You have permission to grow and to step away from those things that no longer fit.

There's a photo of us taken during a paintball game that we clearly did not enjoy. The year was 2011, and we were 29-year-old women who were going through some dark times. Those dark times absolutely shaped our leadership! We were about to step into a wild ride of owning our first company and it all started with a small radio show called, The Girls on the Big Blue Couch Show.

Being called "The Girls" was endearing at first and we totally rocked our branding, but eventually it became something else.

It felt disrespectful.

Condescending even.

We realized that we couldn't step into the leadership realm with that image, and we needed to take ourselves more seriously.

We had to learn self-respect as business owners and leaders.

We had to work with our own Coach to get clear on our messaging.

And we had to start paying ourselves what we were worth - no exceptions.

It's been a long journey, but the Fearless Feminine Leaders of RAYMA Team that you see on the cover of this book are not the same as the Girls on the Big Blue Couch.

Yes, we still care deeply about helping female leaders step into the shoes of confident, respected leaders with emotional strength and resilience. We still care deeply about helping men and women learn how to work together in harmony in professional environments.

But we are not the same people we were a decade ago. And that's how it should be.

You have permission to grow and to step away from those things that no longer fit.

Embrace the story of your past and thank that version of yourself for getting you to where you are today.

And then...

Proudly step into the shoes of the Fearless Feminine Leader that you are!

~Coach Mandy & Coach Raychel

Notes to myself about today's encouragement:

RAYMA Foundations™

We're on a mission to revolutionize how leadership development is done! Let's talk about the history of leadership training...

In the past, leadership training was typically focused on old school methods of control and the bottom-line mentality and curated by men only. Employees that wanted to focus on team morale and human connection were scoffed at. Women had to fight to be heard and get equal access to quality training. And the underdogs - anyone who was different by any definition - were never respected or valued enough to be invited.

But not anymore. It's time to step into a different legacy of leadership.

RAYMA Foundations™ is leadership training for those who want to inspire positive change, no matter their title, and leave their mark on history with:

- Resilience
- Authenticity
- a Yes mindset
- Motivation
- Assertiveness

Leadership like this transcends the workplace. When you embody RAYMA Foundations™, it transforms your life, your family's life, and the future for generations to come. This is how you leave a legacy that matters.

Bring our RAYMA Foundations™ curriculum to your company or organization - or discover how to become a RAYMA Foundations™ Certified Coach and impact 10,000 leaders in five years - at www.raymafoundations.com.

The Truth Statement® Concept:

Years ago, we developed the Truth Statement® concept to help our clients overcome negative thoughts. Saying a Truth Statement® out loud, two to three times a day for 30 days, is a powerful and simple mindset tool that can help you combat fear, anxiety, and doubt while building your faith.

Other Books by RAYMA Team:

For more books by Mandy B. Anderson, Raychel Perman, and RAYMA Team Media, visit www.raymateammedia.com.

Listen & Subscribe to Our Podcast:

Formerly known as the She Who Overcomes Podcast, the Fearless Feminine Leadership Podcast is a weekly show designed to equip women to be confident, Rockstar Leaders. Find it on Apple Podcasts, Spotify, or at www.raymateam.com.

Let's Connect on Social Media!

Instagram: instagram.com/raymateam
Facebook: facebook.com/raymateam
LinkedIn:
- linkedin.com/in/mandybanderson
- linkedin.com/in/raychel-perman-744319160

About RAYMA Team™

RAYMA Team™, LLC is a life and leadership coaching company located in Bismarck, North Dakota. Co-founders, Mandy B. Anderson and Raychel Perman are Best-Selling Authors, Certified Coaches, and life-long friends on a mission to revolutionize how leadership development is done. Learn more about their books, coaching services, corporate training services, and podcast at www.raymateam.com.

ABOUT THE AUTHORS

Mandy B. Anderson

Mandy B. Anderson is the Co-Founder of RAYMA Team™, LLC, a Certified Executive Coach, Award-Winning Author, and TEDx Speaker. Born with a life-threatening disease called Cystic Fibrosis, she has devoted her life to turning disappointments into meaningful experiences and overcoming the obstacles life throws at her.

With nearly a decade of experience in the coaching industry, she specializes in helping leaders navigate hard choices, speak up, and get noticed so they can be Rockstar Leaders with bold confidence, strong teams, and healthy businesses.

Anderson lives by the water in North Dakota where she can be found kayaking or biking with her husband, reading her favorite books with a cute mug of coffee, or adventuring in the park with their fur baby, Indigo – a petite goldendoodle with a big personality. Watch her TEDx Talk and learn how to work with her at www.mandybanderson.com.

ABOUT THE AUTHORS

Raychel Perman

Raychel Perman is the Co-Founder of RAYMA Team™, LLC, a Certified Professional Life Coach, Best Selling Author, Licensed Esthetician, and holds a Bachelor of Science degree in Psychology and Christian Counseling from Liberty University.

As an entrepreneur with the heart of a teacher, she believes that brokenness, trauma, health challenges, and past mistakes do not disqualify you from living and leading well. They prepare you. With nearly a decade of experience in the coaching and personal growth industry, she specializes in helping leaders build confidence and resilience so they can lead strong teams and create healthy businesses.

Perman lives in North Dakota with her husband Josh, three children, and three fur babies. When she is not revolutionizing leadership development, you can find her playing taxi to her busy kids, reading a good novel, or digging in her flower beds. She is a coffee lover, gemstone jewelry collector, obsessed with Britain's royal families, and a big fan of rocking the boat. Learn how to work with her at www.raychelperman.com.

Made in the USA
Columbia, SC
23 January 2023

10940399R00085